How Are They Made?
Helmets

Wendy Blaxland

Marshall Cavendish
Benchmark

New York

Website: www.marshallcavendish.us

This publication represents the opinions and views of the author based on Wendy Blaxland's personal experience, knowledge, and research. The information in this book serves as a general guide only. The author and publisher have used their best efforts in preparing this book and disclaim liability rising directly and indirectly from the use and application of this book.

Other Marshall Cavendish Offices:
Marshall Cavendish Ltd. 5th Floor, 32-38 Saffron Hill, London EC1N 8 FH, UK • Marshall Cavendish International (Asia) Private Limited, 1 New Industrial Road, Singapore 536196 • Marshall Cavendish International (Thailand) Co Ltd. 253 Asoke, 12th Flr, Sukhumvit 21 Road, Klongtoey Nua, Wattana, Bangkok 10110, Thailand • Marshall Cavendish (Malaysia) Sdn Bhd, Times Subang, Lot 46, Subang Hi-Tech Industrial Park, Batu Tiga, 40000 Shah Alam, Selangor Darul Ehsan, Malaysia

Marshall Cavendish is a trademark of Times Publishing Limited

All websites were available and accurate when this book was sent to press.

Library of Congress Cataloging-in-Publication Data

Blaxland, Wendy.
    Helmets / Wendy Blaxland.
      p. cm. — (How are they made?)
    Includes index.
    Summary: "Discusses how helmets are made"—Provided by publisher.
    ISBN 978-0-7614-4755-9
    1. Helmets—Design and construction—Juvenile literature. 2. Plastics--Juvenile literature. I. Title.
    TP1185.H4B585 2011
621.9'92--dc22
                                                                    2009039881

First published in 2010 by
MACMILLAN EDUCATION AUSTRALIA PTY LTD
15–19 Claremont Street, South Yarra 3141

Visit our website at www.macmillan.com.au or go directly to www.macmillanlibrary.com.au

Associated companies and representatives throughout the world.

Copyright © Wendy Blaxland 2010

Edited by Anna Fern
Text and cover design by Cristina Neri, Canary Graphic Design
Page layout by Peggy Bampton, Relish Graphic
Photo research by Jes Senbergs
Map by Damien Demaj, DEMAP; modified by Cristina Neri, Canary Graphic Design

Printed in the United States

Acknowledgments
The author would like to thank the following for their expert advice: Dean Bell, builder of the first children's safety helmet; Peter Bury, Plastics and Chemicals Industries Association, Abbotsford, Victoria, Australia; Randy Swart, Bicycle Safety Helmet Institute, Arlington, Virginia, United States.

The author and the publisher are grateful to the following for permission to reproduce copyright material:

Front cover photographs: Army helmet, Vika Valter/istockphoto (top left); yellow construction helmet, © Kristian Stensønes/ istockphoto (top right); green bike helmet, Zts/istockphoto (bottom left); red motorcycle helmet, © Matthew Cole/istockphoto (bottom right).

Photographs courtesy of:
AFX Helmets, **18**, **19** (top), **20**, **22**, **28**; © Werner Forman/Corbis, **6**; © Owen Franken/Corbis, **7**; © Christel Gerstenberg/Corbis, **27**; © Charles O'Rear/Corbis, **17** (top); Rob Cruse, **25** (bottom); Jim Cummins/Getty Images, **4**; Ferenc Isza/Getty Images, **29**; Brasil2/iStockphoto, **14**; Matthew Cole/iStockphoto, **3** (top), **12**, **19** (bottom); Daydream Girl/iStockphoto, **10**; Gio Adventures/ iStockphoto, **9**; Don Nicolls/iStockphoto, **8**; J. Smith/iStockphoto, **26**; Kristian Stensønes/iStockphoto, **25** (top); Elena Thewise/ iStockphoto, **30**; Vika Valter/iStockphoto, **3** (middle), **11** (bottom); Zts/iStockphoto, **3** (bottom), **13**, **17** (bottom), **21**; Lids on Kids, **24**; NASA, **5**; © Oleksiy Maksymenko/Alamy/Photolibrary, **23**; Paul Rapson/Science Photo Library/Photolibrary, **16**; Snell, **11** (top).

While every care has been taken to trace and acknowledge copyright, the publisher tenders their apologies for any accidental infringement where copyright has proved untraceable. Where the attempt has been unsuccessful, the publisher welcomes information that would redress the situation.

Contents

Glossary Words

When a word is printed in **bold**, you can look up its meaning in the Glossary on page 31.

From Raw Materials to Products

Everything we use is made from raw materials from Earth. These are called natural resources. People take natural resources and make them into useful products.

Helmets

A helmet is a covering for the head to prevent the skull and brain from being damaged in dangerous situations or when traveling quickly. Some helmets also protect the face from wind, light, and dust with a **visor**. Other helmets are fully enclosed to prevent dust or dangerous substances from being breathed in.

Helmets were first made of metal. Modern helmets have a hard shell and a lining designed to take the force of hitting something. The main raw material for making helmets is a range of plastics. Metal and paints may also be used, along with woven polypropylene or nylon in the straps. Modern soldiers' helmets are often made of Kevlar, a light, strong **synthetic** fabric.

Helmets are worn to prevent head injuries while working and playing.

Guess What!

A space helmet is a clear plastic sphere with shields and a tinted visor attached to it. Communication equipment is fastened to the astronaut's head. Space helmets include a strip of rough Velcro so astronauts can scratch an itchy nose.

The first space helmets fitted closely and moved with the astronaut's head. In later helmets, the astronaut could move his or her head freely inside the helmet.

Why Do We Need Helmets?

Helmets are worn to protect the head from injury. Helmets are used in sports such as football and rock climbing, for dangerous work such as mining, and by people riding bicycles and motorcycles. Soldiers wear them, too. Protective helmets are also used in space and underwater, and near dangerous chemicals or infectious diseases that can easily spread.

The History of Helmets

Soldiers have been using helmets for thousands of years to protect their heads from injury during battle. Over the past fifty years, helmets have become an important safety item for motorcyclists and bicycle riders, and also in workplaces such as mines and building sites. After the 1990s, various places made laws about wearing bicycle and motorcycle helmets. However, some people think they should be able to choose whether to wear them or not.

Helmets through the Ages

3000 BCE–400 CE
Helmets are made of leather, then of bronze and iron.

500–1000 CE
European combat helmets called *spangenhelms* are made of leather.

1200
European soldiers wear a flat-topped metal cylinder that completely covers the head over a leather skullcap.

900–700 BCE
Assyrian warriors wear helmets, then Greeks and Romans do.

1400s
Cone-shaped iron and steel helmets develop in Persia, Turkey, and India.

3000 BCE   900 BCE   1 CE   500   1200   1400

This bronze and steel helmet was made in around 600 CE by Vikings in Sweden.

6

A Vietnamese soldier wears a pith helmet.

1970
The Snell Memorial Foundation, an organization that develops helmet safety standards, introduces the first **standard** for helmets.

1989
Australia introduces the world's first compulsory bicycle helmet laws.

1842
The Prussian king Frederick designs the *pickelhaube* ("pointed hat") made of leather boiled to harden it.

1935
The first **compulsory** helmets are used at the Motor Speedway Indianapolis.

1500

1700

1800

1900

2000

1500
European soldiers wear lighter helmets with visors that can be lifted, as part of full suits of armor.

1915
Helmets are introduced to protect soldiers from bomb fragments during World War I.

1966
The first full-face motorcycle helmet is developed.

1991
The **World Health Organization** encourages the use of helmets worldwide.

What Are Helmets Made From?

The outer shell of a helmet can be made of plastic **reinforced** with fibers, which is very strong, yet lightweight. Other shells are made of heavier **thermoplastics**, which melt when heated so they can be molded into shape. Polyethylene, polypropylene, polystyrene, polycarbonate, and nylon are all thermoplastics used in helmets. The inside lining of helmets is made of expanded foams to absorb the force of any blow. Visor shields are usually made of strong, clear, polycarbonate plastic.

Question & Answer

Why do welders wear helmets?

Welders melt metal pieces to join them together. Helmets protect welders from the very bright light, sparks, and unhealthy gases produced. Modern welding helmets have a small visor that darkens automatically.

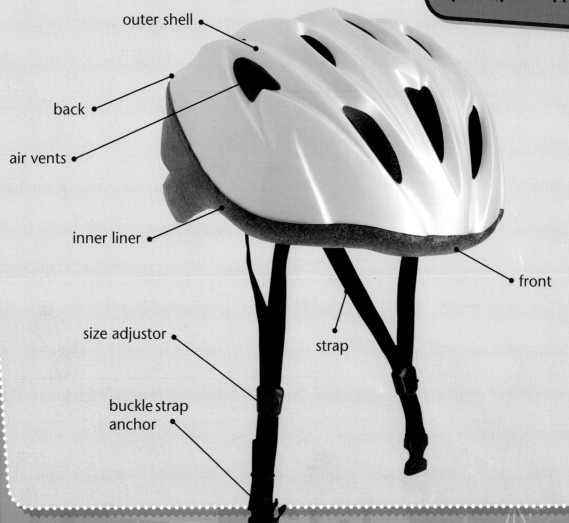

outer shell

back

air vents

inner liner

front

size adjustor

strap

buckle strap anchor

Materials

Helmets are made from a range of plastics with different qualities. As with the making of all products, energy is also used to run the machines that mine the oil and natural gas from which plastics are made, **manufacture** the plastics, and assemble the helmets.

Materials Used to Make Helmets

Material	Purpose and Qualities
Fiber-reinforced plastic	Plastic reinforced with fibers such as carbon or glass makes a strong, light helmet shell that absorbs and spreads **impact**.
Polycarbonate plastic	Used in helmet shells and face shields, polycarbonate is see-through and scratchproof.
Polystyrene, polypropylene, polyurethane	Stiff, light foams used for helmet linings to absorb impact.
Polyethylene plastic	Used in straps and shells, polyethylene is cheap, **flexible**, and long-lasting.
Paints, lacquers, and varnishes	Used to decorate and protect the helmet.
Kevlar	A very strong synthetic fabric used in combat helmets and a few bicycle helmets.
Nylon	Used in chin straps and to cover padding.
Stainless steel	Used in buckles and to reinforce shells, since it does not rust.

This full-face motorcycle helmet has a polycarbonate visor to protect the rider from sun, wind, and airborne objects.

9

Helmet Design

Helmets are designed differently for various purposes. Workers' hard hats contain space on top to absorb the force of falling objects. Communications equipment is built into some sports helmets. The most protective motorcycle helmets and downhill mountain bike racing helmets include chin bars and visors to keep the whole head safe.

Each sport needs a slightly different type of helmet. Football helmets are designed to take repeated hits, hockey helmets need to absorb sharp **shocks**, and batting helmets have earflaps. Helmets for bicycle or motorcycle racing are designed to slice easily through the air.

Designers constantly experiment to improve the way helmets work, and to attract buyers. They often use computer-aided design. Helmets can be also specially decorated with customers' own photos or designs.

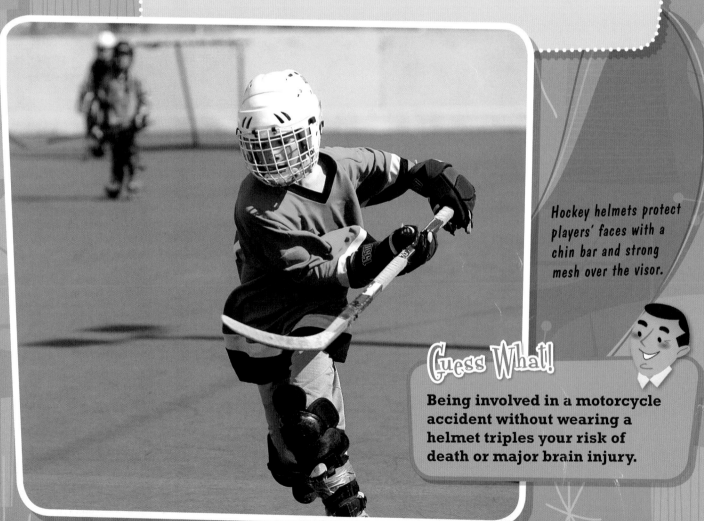

Hockey helmets protect players' faces with a chin bar and strong mesh over the visor.

Guess What!

Being involved in a motorcycle accident without wearing a helmet triples your risk of death or major brain injury.

10

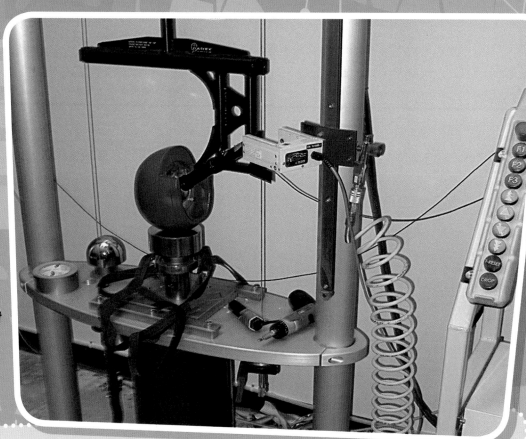

In some countries, helmet designs must be tested to receive approval from a safety authority.

How Do Helmets Work?

Helmets protect heads by absorbing shocks. Head injuries mostly occur to the brain, which is tossed around inside the skull, stretching and bruising brain tissues and tearing blood vessels. Some helmets for certain sports are designed to protect the head from many small shocks.

The hard outer shell on some helmets stops objects from piercing it and holds the lining together. The helmet's inner lining must be squishy enough to slow the head down gently, but be stiff enough to absorb the impact. In some helmets designed for bicycle and motorcycle riding, the lining crushes in an accident, so it is important to replace it afterward.

Crash Testing

Helmets are crash-tested to make sure they work. The helmet is fitted over a head-shaped form that can measure the effect of impacts. Then it is turned upside down and dropped from a range of heights onto hard surfaces that may be flat, curved, or edged, like the different surfaces that helmets can hit.

From Plastic to Helmets

The process of making a helmet involves a number of steps. In the first stage, plastic is made from natural gas, oil, or plants. In the second stage, the outer shell of the helmet is made from hard plastic, and the inner lining from plastic foam. Finally, the inner and outer shells are joined together, the straps and buckles are added, and the helmet is decorated.

Stage 1: Making Plastic

Oil and natural gas are mined.

↓

Then they are broken down into smaller **molecules** at a **refinery**.

↓

Next, the smaller molecules are formed into long chains called **polymers**.

↓

Last, the raw plastic is made into small beads.

Guess What!

Darth Vader's helmet in *Star Wars* was based on Japanese samurai helmets worn into battle by clan leaders. Modern Japanese families display these helmets during the Boys' Festival in the hope that their boys will grow strong.

Stage 2: Forming the Lining and Outer Shell

To make the lining, plastic beads are heated in a mold with steam and expanded into foam to make the right shape.

↓

The lining may also be made stronger by including other materials.

↓

To make the outer shell, a thin sheet of hard plastic is pressed and heated in a mold.

↓

When it cools, it is the correct shape.

↓

Alternatively, a thin sheet of plastic and polystyrene beads are put together in a mold.

↓

Then heat expands the beads, which take the shape of the outer shell.

↓

Next, unwanted parts of the shell are cut away.

Stage 3: Assembling and Finishing Helmets

First, the lining is glued or taped to the outer shell.

↓

Then helmet straps and buckles are fastened to the helmet.

↓

Next, fitting structures and pads may be added inside.

↓

Finally, the helmet is decorated and varnished.

Raw Materials for Helmets

The different plastics used for helmets are all made from oil and gas produced by the **petrochemical industry**. Major petrochemical producers are found in the United States, western Europe, the Middle East, and Asia.

Plastics can also be made from plant materials. At the moment, only one percent of plastic is made from plants. Their use and the demand for them, however, is steadily growing.

Plastics are generally produced by large companies that operate worldwide. China produces most plastic for helmets.

The oil and gas for plastics are mined from under the ground or under the sea floor.

Canada ✳

NORTH AMERICA

United States of America
💧 ✳ ⬦

Mexico ■

ATLANTIC OCEAN

PACIFIC OCEAN

SOUTH AMERICA

Helmets Around the World

More than half of the world's bicycle helmets are now made in China. Many are still assembled in the United States and Europe, however, due to the high cost of shipping them from Asia.

Helmets are used worldwide, especially in the many countries that have passed laws about this, and in sports where helmet wearing is compulsory. Some people object to being forced to wear helmets, despite evidence that they help reduce head injuries and death.

This map shows countries that are important to the production of helmets.

Question & Answer

What are nurdles?

The plastic pellets from which plastic objects are made are called nurdles. A single nurdle is usually less than 0.2 inches (5 millimeters) in diameter.

Key

- ⬩ Important oil-producing countries
- ✳ Important natural-gas–producing countries
- ■ Important plastic-producing countries
- ⛑ Important helmet-manufacturing countries

Russian Federation ⬩ ✳

EUROPE

European Union ✳

Germany ■

ASIA

Spain ■   Italy ⛑

Iran ⬩ ✳

China ⬩ ⛑   South Korea ■ ⛑

Saudi Arabia ⬩   India ■   Taiwan ⛑

PACIFIC OCEAN

AFRICA

ATLANTIC OCEAN

INDIAN OCEAN   AUSTRALIA

Stage 1: Making Plastic

To make plastic, oil and natural gas are first mined from the ground or under the sea. They are taken to a petrochemical refinery. Here, the oil and gas molecules are heated in machines called reactors to break them down. These smaller molecules are then formed into long chains called polymers. Different combinations of polymers and other chemicals produce plastics with different qualities.

Substances are added to the raw polymers to improve their qualities, such as protecting them from sunlight or heat, making them different colors, or expanding them into foam. The raw plastic material is then made into small beads called nurdles.

At the refinery, oil and gas are broken down and made into polymers.

Guess What!

Plastics can also be made from plant substances such as vegetable oil, pea starch, or cornstarch. These bioplastics break down more quickly than other plastics, but are not yet being widely used.

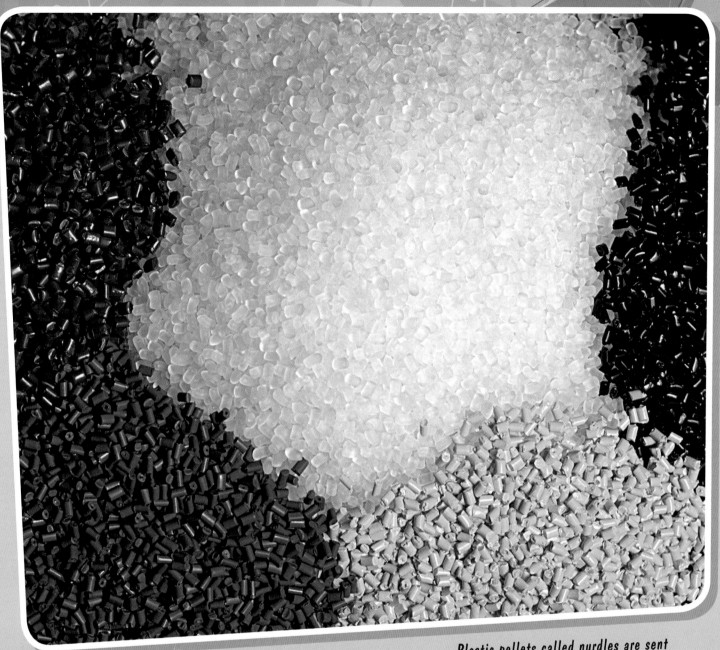

Plastic pellets called nurdles are sent to factories to be made into helmets.

Plastics with Different Qualities

Many plastic polymers are thermoplastic, which means they are softened by heat and become solid again when cooled. Thermoplastics, such as nylon, may be made into thin fibers that can be woven into sheets, and injected or blown into molds to take particular shapes.

Polystyrene beads, about the size of table salt, expand from two to fifty times under pressure and heat to become foam.

Stage 2: Forming the Lining and Outer Shell

The inner and outer shells are made from different plastics.

Forming the Inner Lining

The helmet lining is made by placing beads, usually polystyrene, in a mold and expanding them with steam and pressure into light, stiff but crushable foam. A variety of materials such as nylon, polypropylene, or even metal or metal mesh may be buried in the foam to make it stronger.

Sometimes extra padding is attached to the inner lining of the helmet.

A worker trims unwanted plastic from outer shells of helmets.

Forming the Outer Shell

Inexpensive helmet shells are stamped out from polypropylene and glued or taped to the lining. Helmets may also be made by putting the polystyrene beads inside a thin piece of higher grade plastic, such as polycarbonate, in a mold, and then injecting it with steam under pressure. The steam expands the polystyrene beads into the shape of the mold within the plastic outer shell.

Next, the unwanted parts of the shell are cut away to create vents, mounting holes for the visor, and the visor opening. They may be cut by ordinary blades, water-jet cutting machines, or laser robots.

Question & Answer

Which countries have laws insisting bicycle riders wear helmets?

Bicycle helmets are compulsory in Australia, New Zealand, Finland, Spain, many states in the United States, some provinces in Canada, Iceland, and the Czech Republic (for those under sixteen). Sweden is considering passing such laws. The Union of International Cyclists and USA Cycling insist on helmets in every race they approve.

Stage 3: Assembling and Finishing Helmets

Helmet straps are generally made of woven nylon or polypropylene. Straps are added to the liner before the shell is glued on, or after a helmet has been molded in the shell. They are attached by anchors or are **riveted** on. Buckles are added to hold the straps in place. Different adjustable fitting systems and pads may also be added inside the helmet.

The parts of the helmet are now assembled by hand. The shell may be glued or taped to the lining.

The assembly and finishing of helmets is carried out by hand in factories.

Guess What!

The well-known British policeman's helmet dates back to 1863. It is traditionally made of cork covered by felt or serge fabric, and is 11.8 inches (30 centimeters) tall.

Finishing the Helmet

The helmet may be sanded, painted, polished, and decorated with stickers or painted designs. Often a clear, hard coat of varnish is added to protect the decorations. Stickers with manufacturing information and instructions are added to the inside, and tags that give information about the helmet, style, and manufacturer are attached.

Extras, such as visors, lights, speakers, earmuffs, communication devices, or even a rear-view mirror, may also be added. The helmets are then inspected to make sure everything is correct.

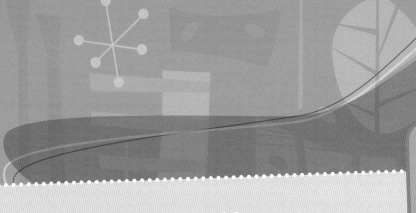

Guess What!

In 2006 the American Bicycle Helmet Safety Institute estimated the cost of an inexpensive bike helmet. Half the cost comes from selling the helmet in the store to a customer.

This chart shows things that contribute to the costs of producing an inexpensive bicycle helmet in the United States.

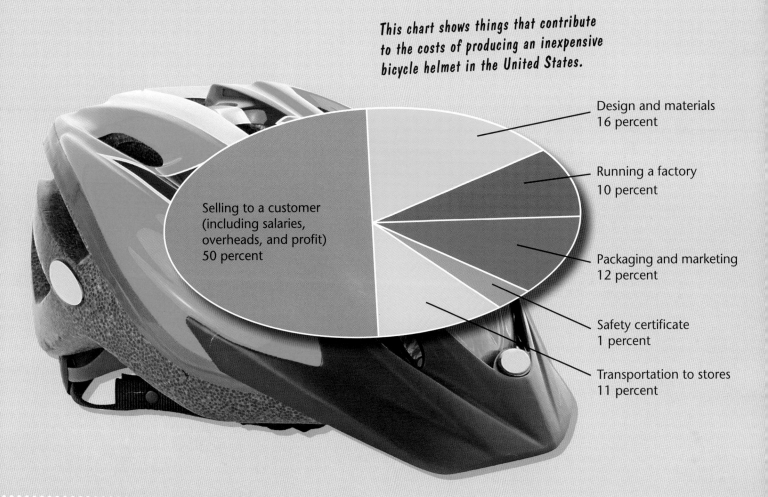

Selling to a customer (including salaries, overheads, and profit)
50 percent

Design and materials
16 percent

Running a factory
10 percent

Packaging and marketing
12 percent

Safety certificate
1 percent

Transportation to stores
11 percent

Packaging and Distribution

Products are packaged to protect them while they are being transported. Packaging also displays the maker's brand and makes products look attractive to customers.

Inexpensive helmets may be packed in plastic or clear cellophane bags, or in a plastic blister pack. More expensive helmets have carefully designed elaborate packaging. Some are cardboard boxes with cut-outs so that customers can see the helmets and try them on. Packaging must protect helmets from scratching, dust, or rough customers.

A number of helmets may then be packed in to a larger box, and perhaps wrapped in plastic. Helmets can also be packed in bulk boxes or crates, or packaged with other extras for a particular sport, such as with kneepads for skateboarding.

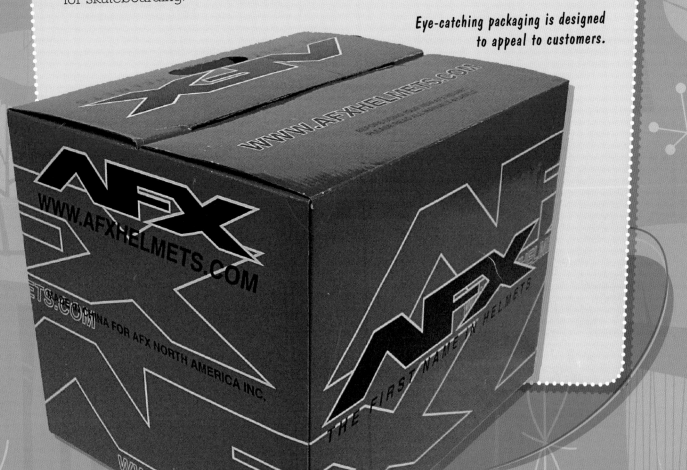

Eye-catching packaging is designed to appeal to customers.

Distribution

Manufacturers generally sell helmets to **distributors** who sell them in a particular region of the world. The helmets are then distributed to **retailers**, such as department stores, chain stores, and bicycle and motorcycle stores, who sell them to individuals. Some helmets are distributed directly over the Internet. Sports teams buy their helmets in bulk, often with special **logos** or colors.

Many bicycle helmets are distributed as a matter of community safety. Charities and local governments may buy and give away helmets or helmet vouchers.

Bright colors and sleek shapes attract buyers' attention.

Guess What!

Diving helmets that seal off the whole of the diver's head were first developed as long ago as 1829 in both England and Russia. They are more secure if a diver becomes unconscious than breathing through a separate mouthpiece, which must be gripped by the teeth.

Marketing and Advertising

Marketing and advertising are used to promote and sell products.

Marketing

Safety is a major selling point for helmets. Many helmet laws have been passed after deaths of people from brain injuries. Helmet-testing institutes, such as the Snell Memorial Foundation in the United States, influence these laws. The foundation is named after Pete Snell, a race-car driver who died in 1956 when his helmet failed to protect him in an accident. In many places, strict safety standards must be met, which are listed on a label inside the helmet.

Helmets are also marketed through educational campaigns promoting safety, in print, and public-service videos. This is common in Southeast Asia, where motorcycles are a major form of transportation. Educational marketing campaigns sometimes encourage people to sign pledges to wear helmets, or they give helmets away.

Question & Answer

What are the effects of helmet laws?

When people understand the difference wearing helmets can make, they generally choose to wear them. When laws make it compulsory to wear helmets, however, many more people wear them. It is estimated that accident deaths are cut by one-third, and injuries are much less severe when people wear helmets.

Stickers from safety organizations promote wearing helmets.

Advertising

Helmets are items of style and fashion for many people. Well-known athletes are paid by helmet manufacturers to wear their products as a form of advertising. Manufacturers give helmet styles names such as "Rage," "Bravo," and "Free Agent" to market a certain image.

Helmets are advertised in sports magazines and store catalogs, and on the Internet. Mini-helmets of sports teams are sold as collectible souvenirs. They become advertising themselves for the real helmets.

Guess What!

A more expensive helmet is not necessarily safer, but it is generally lighter and cooler, and may fit better.

Advertising in special cycling magazines can target customers who are most likely to be interested in helmets.

Production of Helmets

Products can be made in factories in huge quantities. This is called mass production. They may also be made in small quantities by hand, by skilled craftspeople.

Mass Production

Most helmets are mass-produced in large factories in China and Southeast Asia. Some more expensive helmets, however, are designed and manufactured in the United States and Europe, especially Italy. **Specialized** helmets are also made in a number of places.

Making helmets in large numbers enables them to be sold more cheaply. This is important, as it enables helmets to be used as widely as possible. Factories may produce a variety of helmets for different purposes, and different styles are produced only for a certain length of time.

Question & Answer

What is a leatherhead?

This is the name for old-fashioned leather helmets worn by American firefighters. It has also come to refer to the firefighters themselves. The leatherhead is an international symbol for firefighters.

This American firefighter can be identified by the number on his leatherhead helmet.

Small-Scale Production

Helmets can be custom-made for a particular person or purpose. These may be marketed and ordered over the Internet. Often people order expensive helmets specially decorated by hand to show their personality. Athletes also experiment with the look of a helmet or the way it works for their particular sport. There are even helmets for motorcycle-riding dogs!

Some people collect helmets, including those from certain historical periods such as World War I, those worn by particular people or sports teams, or those from a certain manufacturer. Helmets in their original packaging are especially prized.

Helmets can also be produced as gimmicks. Orange helmets in the shape of German World War II helmets made for Dutch fans to wear in a World Cup Soccer match between Germany and Holland aroused strong emotions.

Some helmets, such as this German military helmet from the 1870s, are prized by collectors and museums for their historical value.

Helmets and the Environment

Making any product affects the environment. It also affects the people who make the product. It is important to think about the impact of a product through its entire life cycle. This includes getting the raw materials, making the product, and disposing of it. Any problems need to be worked on so products can be made in the best ways possible.

Plastics

Plastic for helmets is mainly made from oil and natural gas. These are **nonrenewable resources**, which will eventually run out. Plastics made from plants are a possible **renewable** alternative. Responsible employers protect plastics workers dealing with dangerous chemicals. Plastic breaks down into tiny particles which can carry toxic chemicals, but does not decay. Plastic has created a worldwide pollution problem.

Some chemicals can be a hazard to people who work with plastics.

Recycling

Helmets are made of different forms of plastic. The different types of plastic must be sorted for recycling, which is why not much plastic is recycled. High-density polyethylene, however, can be recycled into items such as park benches. Some mixed plastic can be used to help make road surfacing, or as a source of carbon in recycling scrap steel. It is also possible to break plastic back down into the molecules it was made from to recycle it, or even turn it back into petroleum.

Reusing

Some helmets, such as football helmets, can be checked and reconditioned.

Workers sort containers according to the type of plastic they are made from so that they can be recycled.

Guess What!

In 2008, Daniel Burd, a sixteen-year-old Canadian schoolboy, discovered two sorts of bacteria that, together, can break down polyethylene plastic within three months.

Questions to Think About

We need to conserve the raw materials used to produce even ordinary objects such as helmets. Recycling materials such as plastic, conserving energy, and preventing pollution as much as possible mean there will be enough resources in the future and a cleaner environment.

These are some questions you might like to think about.

* Why are laws passed to make people wear helmets?

* Do you always wear a helmet while cycling or skating?

* Can you think of a good way to recycle helmets in your local community or school?

* What are the benefits and problems with plastics made from plants?

* What are the benefits and disadvantages of biodegradable plastics?

* What does your favorite helmet look like?

Helmets save lives.

Glossary

compulsory
Required.

distributors
Sellers of large quantities of goods that have the right to sell a particular product in a certain area.

flexible
Able to bend.

impact
Forceful contact.

logos
Images that represent company brands.

manufacture
Make, in factories mainly by machine.

molecules
Groups of atoms or tiny particles that make up a substance.

mold
A hollow form in which materials can be shaped to make objects.

nonrenewable resources
Resources that cannot be easily replaced once they run out.

petrochemical industry
The business of manufacturing chemical products from petroleum oil or natural gas.

polymers
Long chains of molecules in substances such as plastic.

refinery
A factory where raw materials are treated to make them purer or more useful.

reinforced
Made stronger.

renewable
Something that can be easily grown or made again.

retailers
Stores that sell products to individual customers.

riveted
Pinned together with a metal stud.

shocks
Sudden, violent collisions.

specialized
Designed for a particular job.

standard
A certain accepted level of quality.

synthetic
Made by humans, often using petrochemicals.

thermoplastics
Plastics that can be softened and shaped when heated and become solid again when cooled.

visor
The front covering on a helmet to protect the face, especially the eyes.

World Health Organization
International health authority that provides leadership on health matters worldwide.

Index